This project was made possible by the generous sponsorship
of the following organizations

Funded from Glasgow District Council's Festivals Budget.

GLASGOW

24 Hours in the Life of a City

CHAPMANS

Chapmans Publishers Ltd
141–143 Drury Lane
London WC2B 5TB

First published by Chapmans 1990

© The Glasgow Shoot Ltd 1990

Photographs © The Photographers 1990

ISBN 1 85592 505 2

Phototypeset in Great Britain by
Input Typesetting Ltd

Colour origination by
Mandarin Offset, Hong Kong

Printed and bound in Singapore

Design and art direction by Graeme Murdoch

Designed and produced on behalf of The Glasgow Shoot Ltd by
Tarbert Enterprises Ltd, The Richmond Business Centre
Richmond, Surrey TW9 1JY

Half-title page photograph by Mike Goldwater : the moment the day began

Title page photograph by Christopher Morris : at 9 pm jubilant fans wave the Scottish flag at Hamden

LET GLASGOW FLOURISH

This book is dedicated to all Glaswegians
wherever they may be

ACKNOWLEDGMENTS

The Project Staff
Project Director – Duncan Howie
Project Manager – Heather Sutherland
Photographic Consultant – Gerard McCann
Research Consultant – Mike Higgins

Photographers' Assistants
Christine Stevenson   Anne McBride
Chris Blott   Alastair McFarlane
Neil Ramsay   Robert Tabor

Picture Editors' Assistants
Davie Sheerin   Stephen Moore
Zoé Kaka   Jon Lee
Des Kodur   Paul Reid

Drivers
Jonathon Fox   Douglas Kenney
Tommy McCanny   William Bell

Photo Shoot Co-ordinators
Mike Higgins   Ally Palmer   Tom McAllister

Researchers
Write Now team
Moray Coulter   Linda Brown   Carol Goldrich

E-Force Glasgow team
(a joint BBC/CSV Media Training Project)
Meg McGuinness   John Farman   Anvar Khan
Margaret Blythe   Linda Duff

Picture Editors
Jocylyn Benzakin (JB Pictures, New York)
Steve Blogg (Telegraph Weekend Magazine)
Colin Jacobson (The Independent Magazine)
Geoff Katz (Katz Pictures, London)
Graeme Murdoch (Scotland on Sunday)
June Stanier (The Observer Magazine)

Black and white prints hand printed by Malk Bruckner

Sponsors, Friends and Helpers

Many people and organisations have helped to make this project a success and The Glasgow Shoot would like to thank the following in particular. Andrew Gaffney of the Professional Photography Division of Kodak Ltd; David Macdonald of Glasgow Action; Renée Gillespie of the West of Scotland Division of British Telecom and staff in the Business Centre at Heron House; Jon Pack of the Public Affairs Department at BP Exploration; David Black and the staff of the Holiday Inn Glasgow; Stewart Mackintosh of Write Now; Steve Brown, manager of E-Force; Joe McGahey and Captain George Muir of Clyde Helicopters; Joe O'Donnell of Ian Skelly Holdings Ltd who supplied transport during the days of the photo-shoot; George Reynolds of Scotrail/Intercity who helped with transport to Glasgow; Angie Boyle who helped arrange travel in London and Margaret Caldes who helped arrange travel in New York; Jill Campbell-Mackay, press officer of the District Council Festivals Unit; Jim Clements and Ian Campbell of the Photography Department at the Glasgow College of Building and Printing and their final year photography students; Andy McCulloch and his staff at B & S Colour Labs; Douglas McGregor and his staff at Clyde Colour Labs; Dave Fairey and Peter Theodosiou for help in London and Tricia Boyle for all her faith and support; finally, all the people and organisations in the City of Glasgow who were so helpful to our researchers and welcoming to our photographers – we hope that you all enjoy the results.

THE PROJECT

Glasgow, the official European City of Culture 1990. The city with a certain reputation, celebrated and notorious, is now being ranked alongside Florence and Athens. *Let Glasgow Flourish* is the city's motto and flourishing it is. In the summer of 1988 Glasgow hosted the Garden Festival and millions of visitors mingled with city residents to enjoy it. Now for a whole year culture in its widest sense is to be enjoyed in the city. From impromptu street theatre to Grand Opera, the ephemeral to the permanent. Not that any of this will surprise the large numbers who attend events during Mayfest, the now well-established month of cultural activity which rivals the Edinburgh Festival in popularity.

To record all this, television programmes have been made, books have been published and newspaper and magazine articles have been written. The Year of Culture like the Garden Festival will come and go but what about everyday life in the city which continues regardless of events like these. That is what this project is about. Taking thirty-three top photo-journalists from Scotland and abroad and giving them over one hundred assignments the objective was to capture in photographs the essence of life in the city for its people. Rushing all over the city between midnight and midnight they were to take over 40000 photographs which, with the help of a panel of top picture editors, were reduced to the best 200 or so of all those taken on the day to be reproduced in this book and exhibited in the city at the end of the year with the twelve best printed in a calendar.

A project like this is expensive and takes a lot of organising and with the idea coming late

The photo-shoot control room
at the Holiday Inn

Photographers noting details for captions

in 1989 we had to decide on a day for the photo-shoot. We wanted an 'ordinary day' but quickly realised that there is no such thing so we settled on Wednesday 28 March, just after the clocks went forward by an hour and just before Easter. In the four months that followed we secured sponsorship to help cover the costs, found a publisher for the book, chose the photographers and researched the assignments. A potential nightmare but with goodwill and co-operation we succeeded. The many people and organisations who contributed to and helped execute the project are listed at the front of this book and in the acknowledgments.

What if it rains on the day was a question often asked, to which the answer was, we carry on. Looking out from our office at falling snow on the week-end before the photo-shoot some doubts crept into that confident reply. We need not have worried. The day itself was one of unbroken sunshine. One photographer even complained that it was too bright; he wanted some clouds!

Whatever day was chosen for this project it was inevitable that there were aspects of life that we were unable to cover. For example on the chosen day the Universities were closed for the Easter Vacation. Though we were intending to record everyday life in the city we could not ignore cultural events which happen throughout the city in normal years. However no orchestras, operas or ballets were in performance on that day nor was there anything on at the Citizen's Theatre. In contrast that evening was dominated by a football international at Hamden Park where, in World Cup year, Scotland beat the reigning World Champions Argentina.

After a long hard day it is time to relax

Thirty-three photographers is a large number to bring to the city and organise but Glasgow is a large city with more than a million people in it during the day and even with this number of photographers it is not possible to take pictures of absolutely everything going on in the city. The assignments were chosen to give as wide a spectrum of life in the city as possible which meant for example choosing representative schools and hospitals from the many in the city and showing contrasting housing, shopping and lifestyles while trying to avoid clichés. The photographers were given an average of four assignments each to cover during the day and were also free to use their

initiative to take advantage of chance opportunities as they arose. Unfortunately this meant that in the excitement of the day some assignments were not covered and we apologise for any inconvenience caused.

Ultimately the vitality of any city lies in its people and this book shows the variety and depth of character of the people of the City of Glasgow.

This is the result of the Glasgow Shoot project and we hope you will enjoy it for a long time to come – you may even be featured in it.

Some of the 40000 photographs taken waiting to be edited.

The team of picture editors voting during the initial edit

THE PHOTOGRAPHS

DAVID MODELL

In the early hours of the morning the working day is just beginning
for the driver of night bus 801 as she takes her passengers home

DAVID MODELL

Happy birthday Diane Carmichael –
photographer Tom Stoddart joined her 18th birthday
party until the wee small hours of the morning

By 4 am Tom had moved on to M & A Brown,
a traditional city bakers
where bread making for the morning is well under way

The Necropolis caught in the eerie half-light of the dawn at 6 am

The Dutch submarine *Potuis* glints in the rapidly rising sun

The sun is fully up by 7.30 am and the Necropolis looks much less daunting

RICHARD WAITE

Steering the Renfrew ferry 6 am

KENNETH JARECKE

Morning deliveries at Wiseman's Dairies, Possil Park 6.30 am

GERARD McCANN

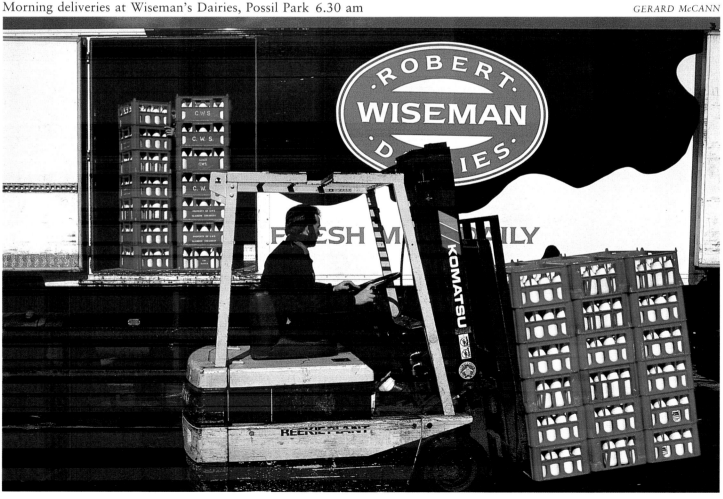

Fruit and veg market, Blochairn 6.30 am
Breakfast with the Sloan family, Drumchapel 8 am

ALEXANDRA AVAKIAN

DAVID MITCHELL

DAVID MODELL

The inner circle on the underground
just before the rush hour starts at 8 am (top and bottom)

DAVID MODELL

One Glaswegian who is not in a rush to go anywhere

Aerial picture of the city at dawn as it wakes and goes to work 8 am

RON ANDERSON

RON ANDERSON

Now the mist has cleared and the photographs on this page and the following page
taken at 9 am, show the two main arteries of the city – the motorway and the river

Putting on the finishing touch, before facing the world – Drumchapel 8.30 am
Three men and a dog have a natter 9 am

MARK PETERSON
MIKE WILKINSON

Argyll Street in the morning

TOM STODDART

Morning cleaner, Hollywood Secondary School 7.30 am

MIKE GOLDWATER

NIGEL PARRY

Between 7 am and 11 am Nigel Parry set up a studio on the concourse of Central Station
and invited passengers to pose for him.

NIGEL PARRY

The photographs on these two and the following two pages are a selection of those who agreed to pose

All photographs by Nigel Parry

All photographs by Nigel Parry

MIKE GOLDWATER

The Chaplin at Hollywood Secondary School prepares to take morning mass

Children study in the Mosque Ramadan begins today.

Grandmother and granddaughter – Jehovah's Witnesses in mid-morning bible study at home

Taking a mid-morning break where Town meets Country on the edge of Drumchapel

MARK PETERSON

Morning exercise for two pit bull terriers in Blackhill 9.30 am

MARC ASNIN

CHRISTOPHER PILLITZ

Dogs and owners wait their turn
at the morning surgery
in the Glasgow Vet School

Morning training at Parkhead for Celtic players

MIKE WILKINSON

Early morning exercise (for some) in Drumchapel

MARK PETERSON

RON ANDERSON

Aerial picture of refurbished towerblocks
with new shapely roofs and painted walls

It was a busy time in the Rottenrow Maternity Hospital
where photographer John Young spent the whole day.
The photographs on these six pages
are a selection from the many he took

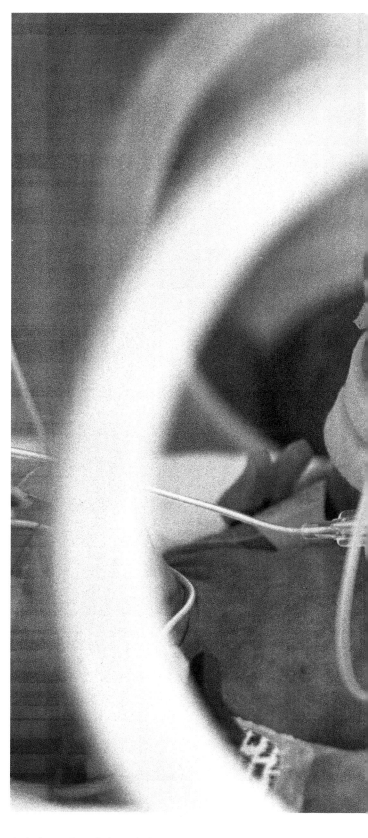

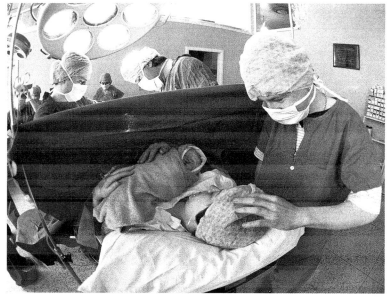

JOHN YOUNG

The delivery room

A father's hand dwarfs his premature baby

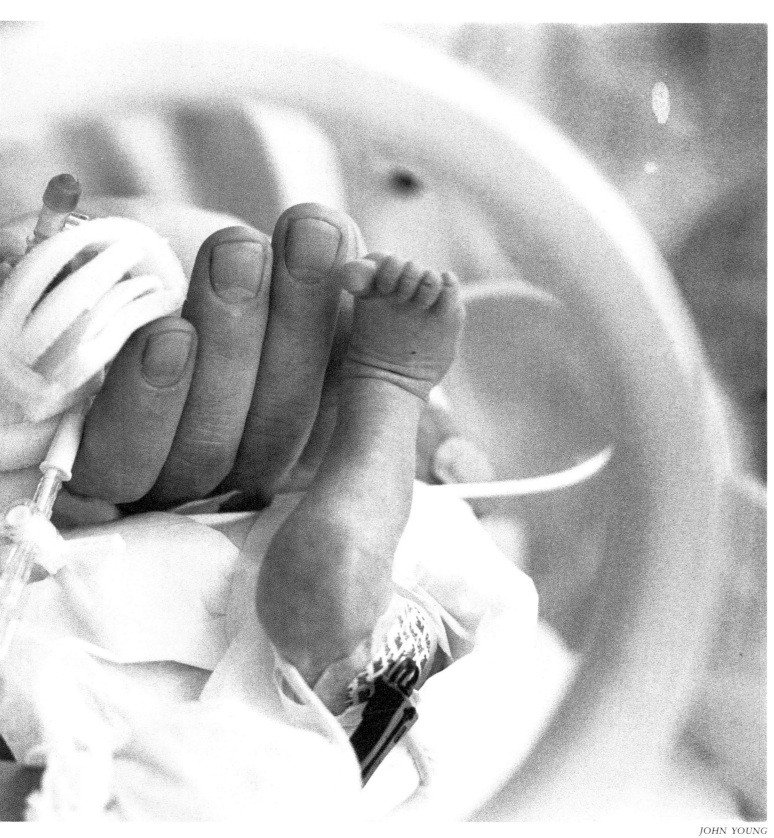

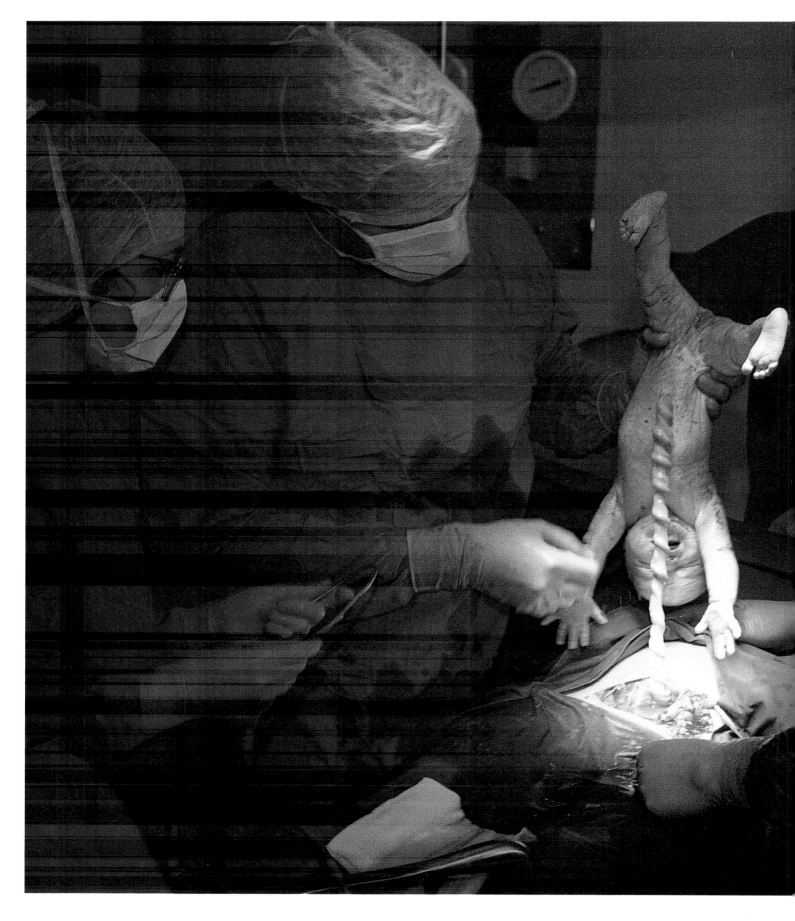

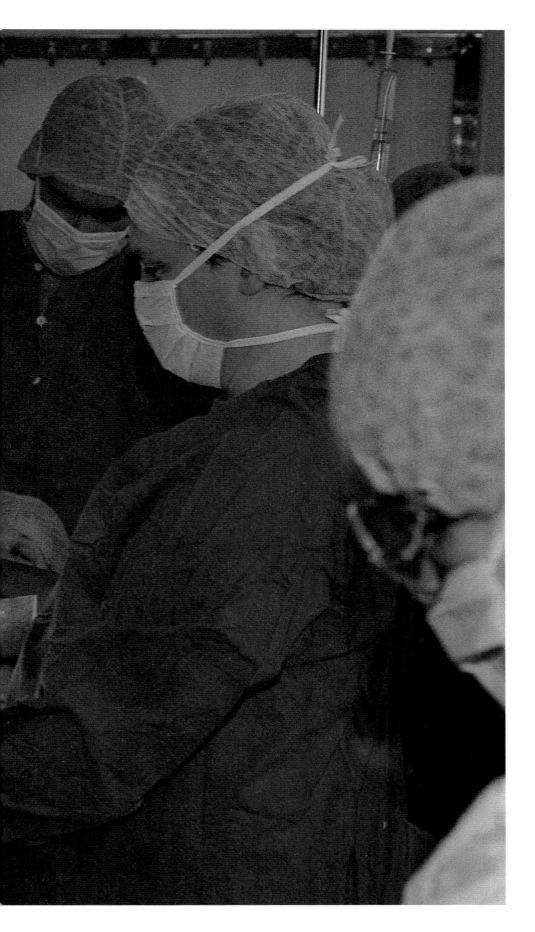

In the operating theatre of
Rottenrow Maternity hospital
at 12.27 pm and Dawn Hutchison,
weighing 3 kilogrammes is born to
Jeanette and Jim from Easterhouse

JOHN YOUNG

Mother and baby
both doing fine

JOHN YOUNG

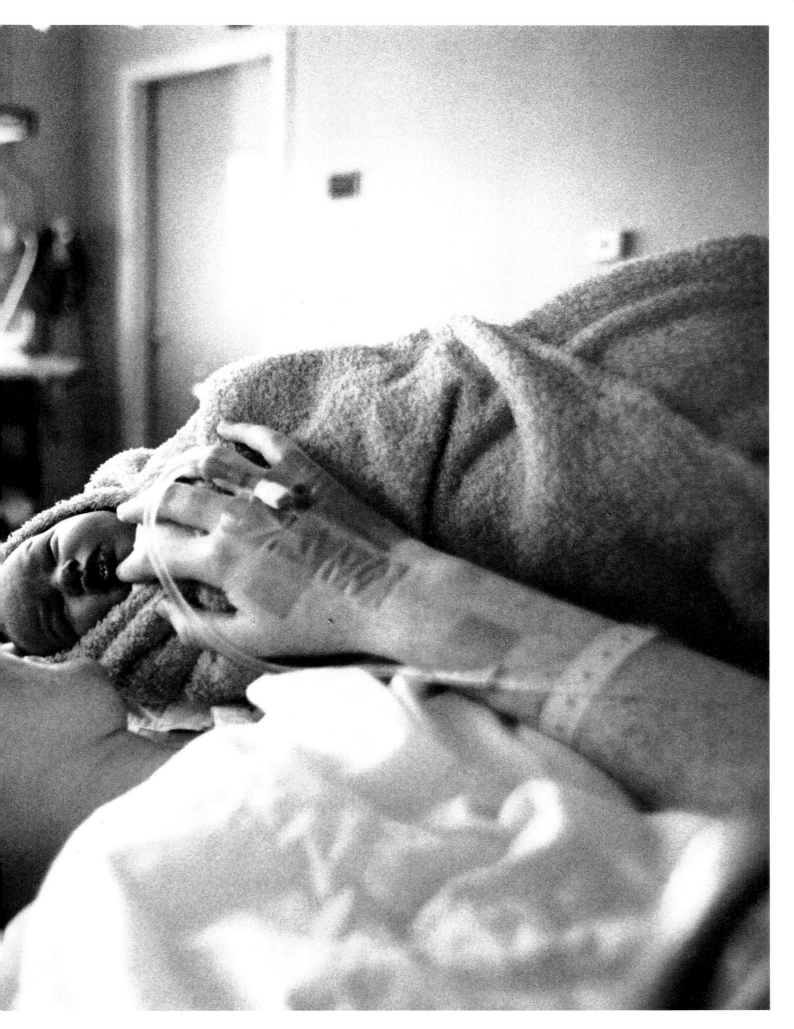

Police stables, Netherpollock Estate

MIKE ABRAHAMS

Animals feature in many Glaswegians' lives both for work and as pets.
Most are loved as is the police horse (left) and the pigeon (bottom).
However, from these pictures taken in the late morning
the one of the puppy tells a less loving story

Cat and Dog Home

CHRISTOPHER MORRIS

GLYN SATTERLEY

George Dunn at the Pigeon Swap Shop

ROBERT GUMPERT

The energy of youth is clear in these two photographs taken just before lunch.
One child was caught in passing leaping from shed top to shed top
in a housing scheme and the other imitating art at the Burrell Collection,
Glasgow's most successful new Museum

NIGEL PARRY

Football in Drumchapel – dreaming of Hamden where Scotland
took the field against Argentina eight hours later that night

MARK PETERSON

Looking out from the new St Enoch Centre onto St Enoch Square

EMILE LUIDER

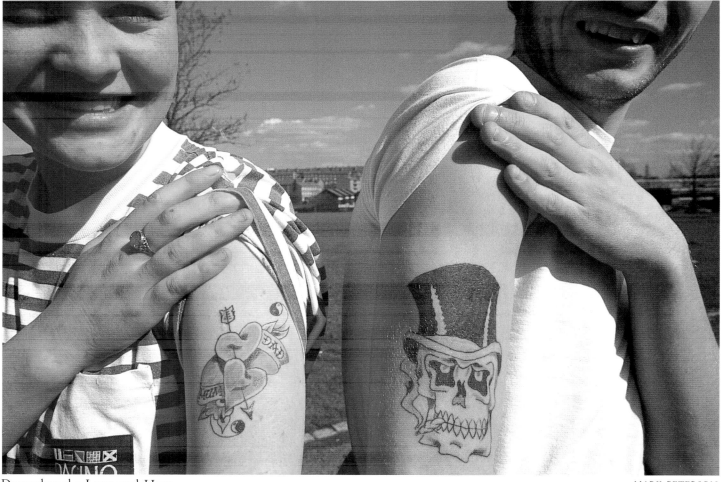

Drumchapel : Love and Hate
A kiss before lunch

MARK PETERSON

GERARD McCANN

Two cool kids in the Gorbals and a security guard
outside the Stock Exchange wear sunglasses in the bright morning sun

TOM STODDART

STEPHEN GIBSON

Contrasts in city housing. Affluent detached houses on the south side of the city (above) and Possil Park (right), an area awaiting regeneration

MIKE ABRAHAMS

RONNIE ANDERSON

MIKE GOLDWATER

Mark Peterson

The grass burning on the edge of the city is deliberate as a way of controlling its growth

Mark Peterson

A young Glaswegian plays on his swing oblivious to the fire behind him

DAVID MITCHELL

Children in the city's hospital whose imagination can turn a wheel-chair
into a go-kart and all respond to love and affection

JOHN DOWNING

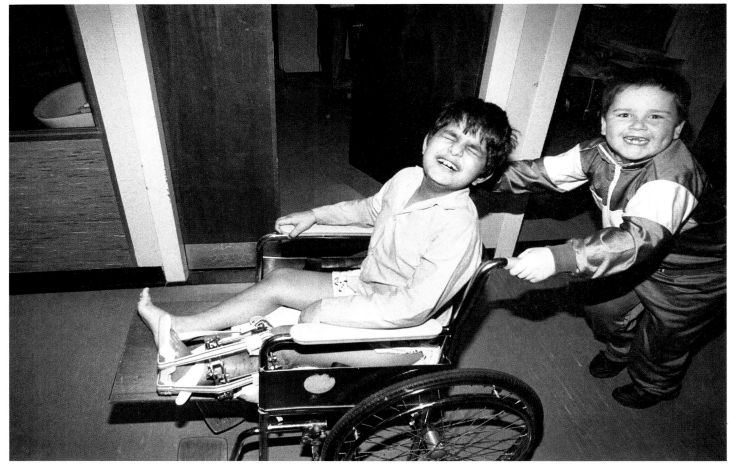

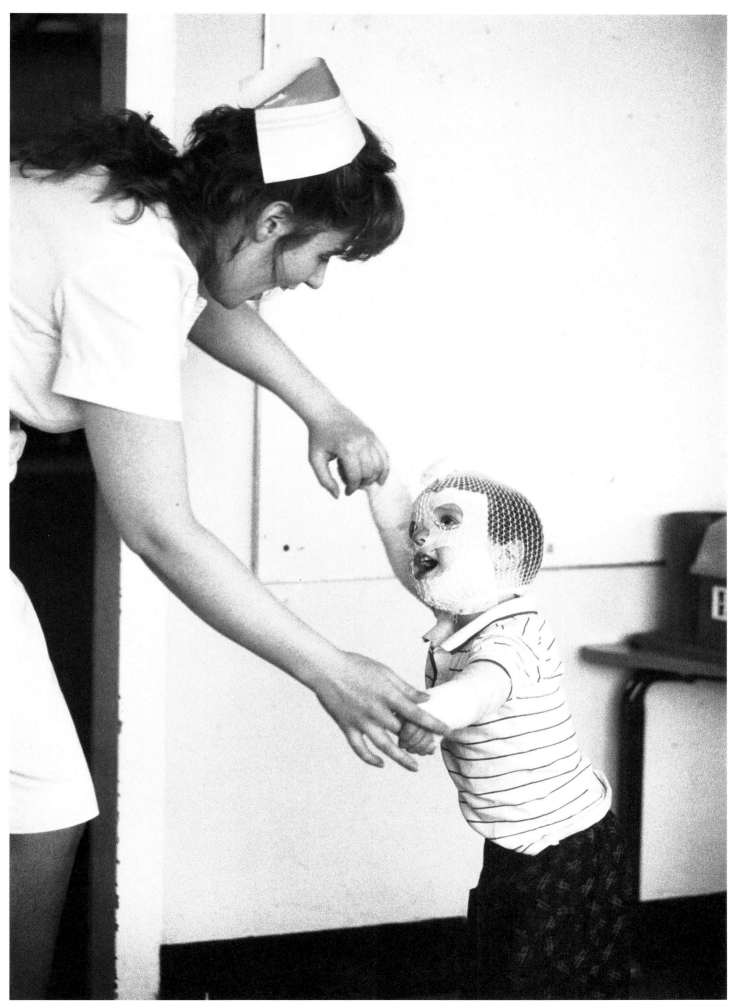

JOHN DOWNING

After visiting the Police stables at Netherpollock Estate in the morning photographer Mike Abrahams took this picture of two officers on patrol in the city

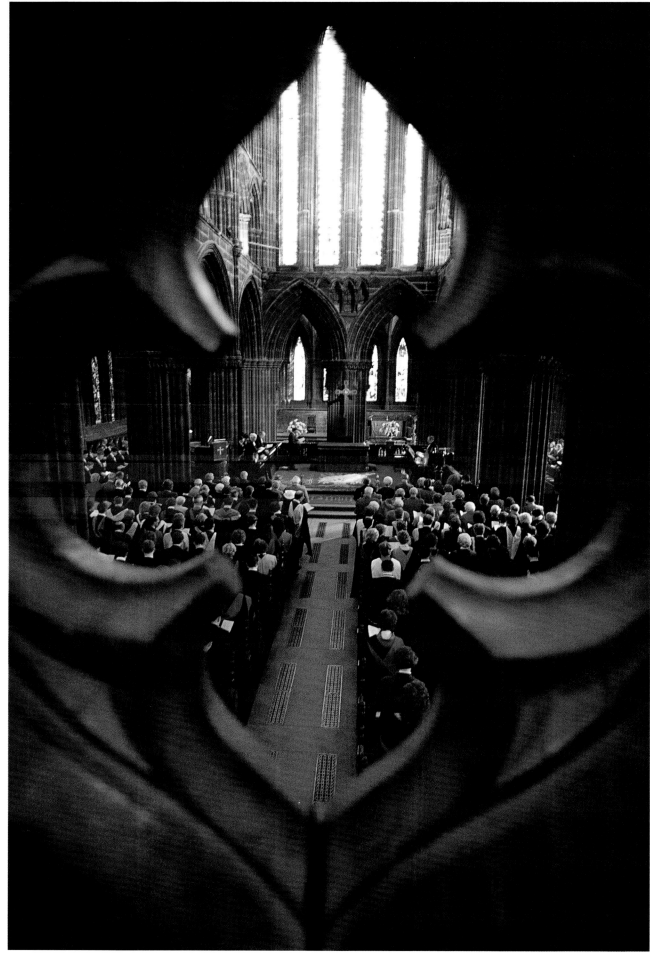

DON MCPHEE

Glasgow Cathedral (above and bottom right).
This morning service was to celebrate founder's day for Hutcheson's Grammar School

Music lesson, Hollywood Secondary School

MIKE GOLDWATER
DON MCPHEE

The photographer missed what the joke was about by stopping to take this picture
of three Glasgow women out shopping at mid-day

NEIL LIBBERT

Drama group, Hollywood Secondary School 11 am
The head of a client at Alan Edward's salon 12 noon

TOM STODDART
MIKE GOLDWATER

DAVID MITCHELL

Between assignments in the middle of the day photographer David Mitchell
caught this outdoor hair salon for dogs run by Robert Walker and John Cameron

It's not all action on television –
taking a break on the set of *Taggart*

The taxidermy workshop
at Kelvingrove Museum

TOM STODDART

DON McPHEE

After a prolonged and vigorous public campaign the Glasgow Vet School was saved.

CHRISTOPHER MORRIS

MIKE ABRAHAMS

Walking the dog in the midday sun
with the Red Road flats
in the background.

The Red Road flats

MIKE ABRAHAMS

Aerial picture of an immaculately kept city cemetery in the mid-day sun.

JILLIAN EDELSTEIN

Margaret Donnigan and Isabel Jarvie, both keen lunchtime swimmers

Ann Grant and Colin Minar at the Holiday Inn swimming pool

Contrasting lunch styles in a
bar in the very fashionable
Merchants' City

DAVID ROSE

MIKE GOLDWATER

Paddy's Market
is full of interesting people

Jamie Barr in the Rosewall Bar
where he entertains the regulars

MICHEL SETBOUN

Glasgow's annual cultural feast, the Mayfest, is only four weeks away
and the first sign goes up on the CO-OP building

The suspension footbridge over the River Clyde

GLYN SATTERLEY

The People's Palace

EMILE LUIDER

EMILE LUIDER

The suspension footbridge over the River Clyde looking north to Clyde Street 12.30 pm

Lunch in the Wintergarden at the People's Palace
on Glasgow Green 1 pm

EMILE LUIDER

MARK PETERSON

Lunchtime at Kingsbridge Secondary School

Clearing up after lunch in the afternoon at 1 Devonshire Gardens
before beginning preparations for dinner

MIKE GOLDWATER

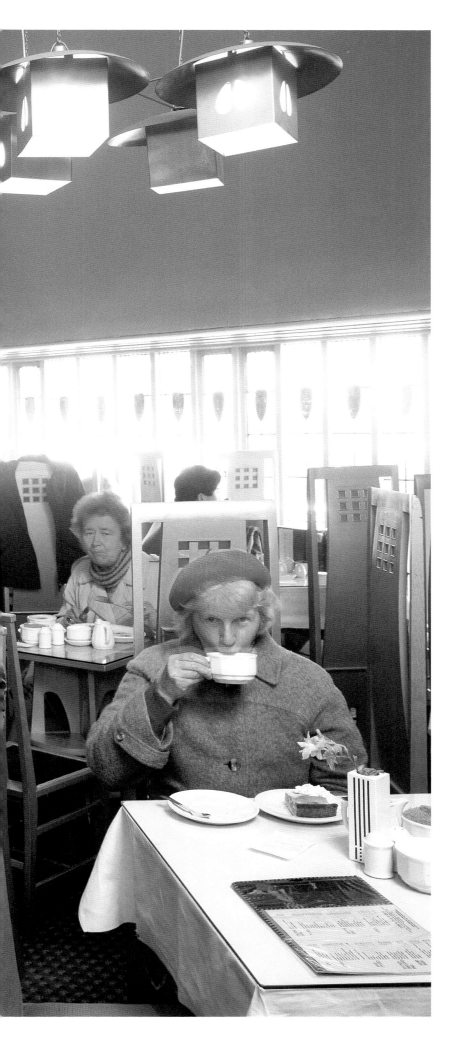

Lunch is about to be served at
the Willow Tea Rooms, Sauchiehall Street

RICHARD WAITE

DAVID ROSE

The footbridge over the Clyde is almost deserted in the middle of the day
unlike the parked cars below the motorway in the city centre
which seem almost to huddle together for warmth

On pages 96 and 97 are contrasting styles of housing.
Page 96 shows high-rise flats in the background
and St. Georges Church Woodside, recently converted into flats.
Page 97 shows pigeons housed in George Reilly's bedroom.

Artistic talent in Glasgow is blooming

LESLEY DONALD

A small child is dwarfed by the interior
of the new Princes Square shopping centre

KENNETH JARECKE

City street scene

Young travelling person at a site in Possilpark

STEPHEN GIBSON

MIKE GOLDWATER

Science lesson, Hollywood School

A late lunch in Princes Square

IAN HOSSACK

Two friends pictured enjoying the warm afternoon sun

CHRISTOPHER MORRIS

Christine Ironside, artist in residence at the Botanical Gardens

GLYN SATTERLEY

TOM STODDART

A solitary cup of tea at the St. Enoch Centre 3 pm

Blackhill

Boys and girls

MARC ASNIN

ALEXANDRA AVAKIAN

George Square

IAN HOSSACK

A contrast in shopping styles.
Whatever was bought in Princes Square in the afternoon it was not junk

Tam Shephard's Magic Shop, Queen Street 3 pm

IAN HOSSACK

In the afternoon sun
Up For Grabs perform in Buchanan Street

Looking in on the St Enoch Centre

EMILE LUIDER

Good at Sports   likes music   Needs surveillance

IAN BERRY

A more serious photograph highlighting
the most contentious political argument of the year

Young Glaswegians in the afternoon

MARK PETERSON

Steve Blair from Drumchapel

Paddy's market 4 pm

IAN HOSSACK

MARC ASNIN

Blackhill

Two powerful portraits of young Glaswegians in the afternoon

CHRISTOPHER PILLITZ

The Victoria Bar

Lydia Farrell having her hair done
by Alan Edwards in his salon
at the Briggait 3 pm

TOM STODDART

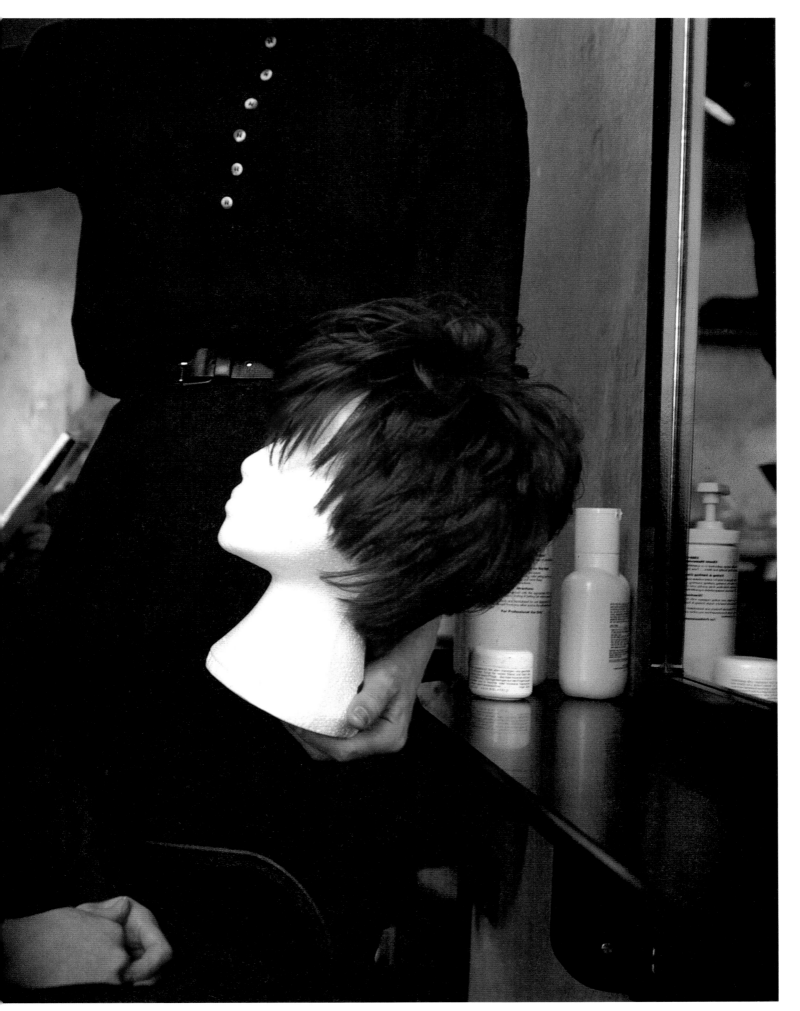

NEIL LIBBERT

A young Jehovah's Witness at Kingdom Hall
in the afternoon break

This Aladdin's cave is near the Briggait Centre

Looking to see what's on television – not much

You can find anything you want at Paddy's Market

Terry the Tattoist –
Stuart Wrigley works on
a client while her
boyfriend waits

ALEXANDRA AVAKIAN

Glasgow tenements in Possilpark

The Western Infirmary, accident and emergency unit

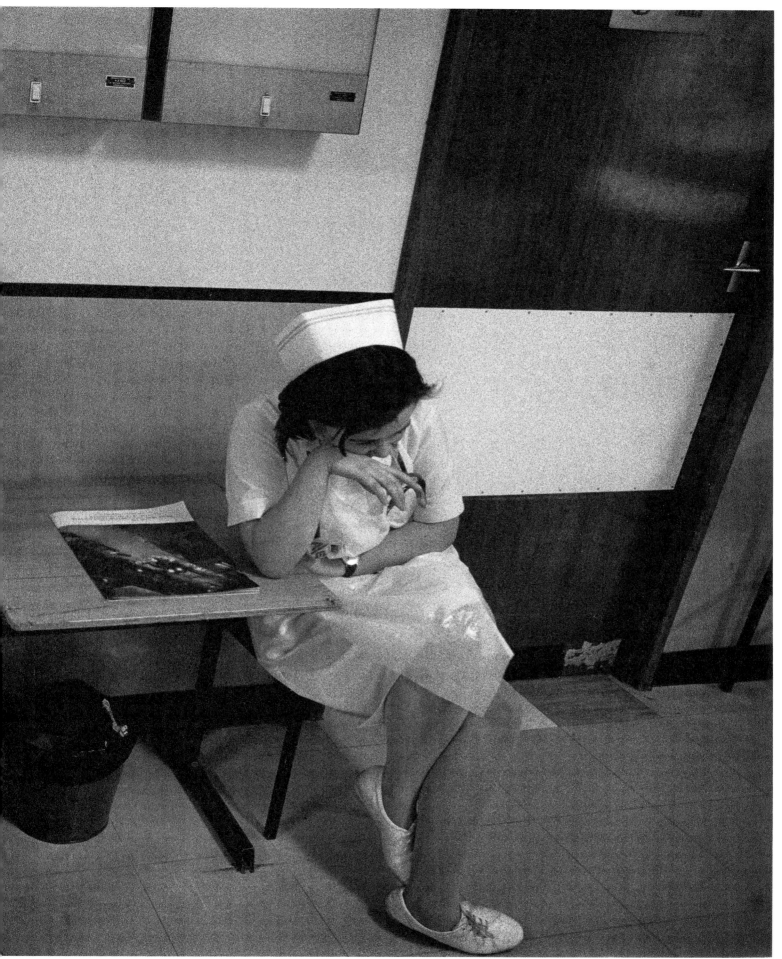

ALEXANDRA AVAKIAN

ALLAN MILLIGAN

George Graham with Roddy the hamster, Easterhouse

On the way home after school ends for the day 4 pm

CHRISTOPHER MORRIS

Three girls from Garnetbank School

EMILE LUIDER

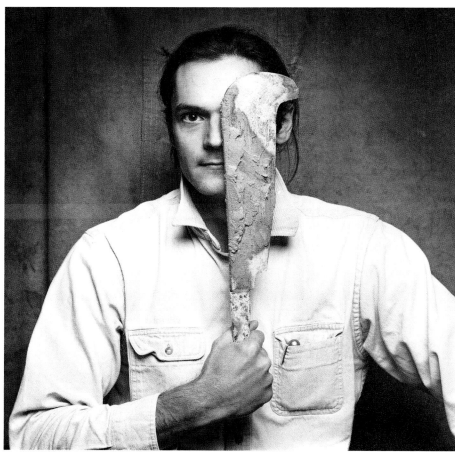

NIGEL PARRY

A poseur poses – artistically in the afternoon
Glasgow Sculptor Studies

Art study at the Burrell Collection

NIGEL PARRY

KENNETH JARECKE

Lord Provost Susan Baird during a busy day.
Next appointment was with the Mayor of Berlin

JILLIAN EDELSTEIN

Lady Alice Barnes (seated at front) and friends take afternoon tea

Afternoon tea dancing
at Carringtons OAP club

IAN BERRY

IAN BERRY

Ballroom dancing is very popular in Glasgow,
as the picture on the previous pages and these two pages show

Ballroom Dancing at the Mayfair, Sauchiehall Street

IAN BERRY

Student street theatre, Central Station 5 pm

Punjabi folk dancing Kinning Park 6 pm

ALEXANDRA AVAKIAN

Lini Djatmiko and her son Ellinas enjoy the late afternoon sun
while feeding pigeons in George Square

MIKE GOLDWATER

GERARD McCANN

Working out in the Gym

Football is not the only form of exercise taken in Glasgow,
as these early evening pictures show

Tae Kwan Do, Eastbank Academy, Shettleston

IAN HOSSACK

Almost time to go home for this security guard outside
the Argyll Arcade at 5.50 pm.

GLYN SATTERLEY

Contrasting rivers flow through the city.
The river Kelvin (top) and the river Clyde (bottom)

KENNETH JARECKE

Kvaerner shipyard, Govan

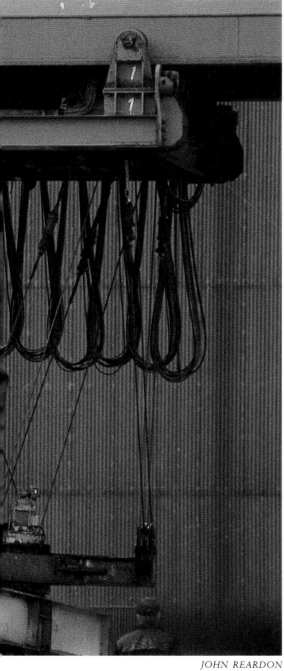

RICHARD WAITE

Three workers at Howden Engineering

JOHN REARDON

MIKE GOLDWATER

Something to look forward to after work

Home at the end of the day

The party started early tonight

Time to go home for these school pupils

Parachute training with the Territorial Army, Maryhill

JOHN DOWNING

A bath, a shave and early to bed
at the Talbot Centre for the single homeless (pages 158 to 161)

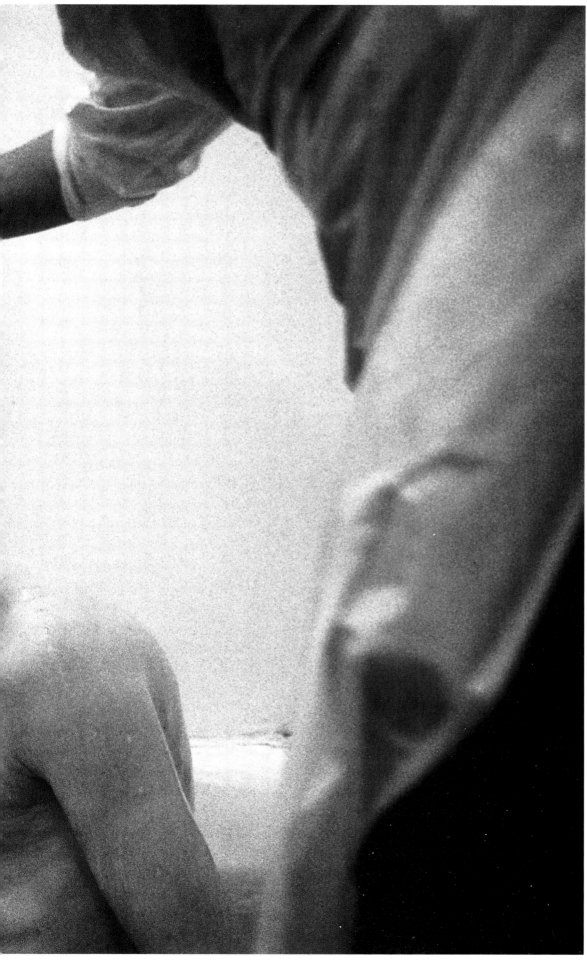

JOHN REARDON

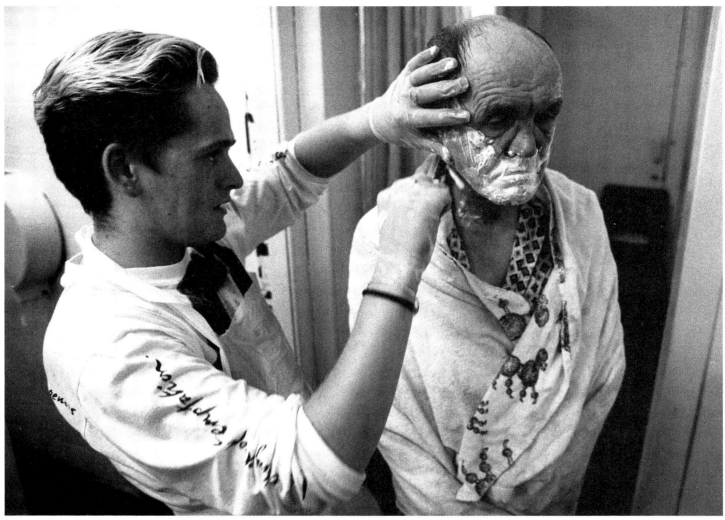

JOHN REARDON

Talbot Centre for the single homeless   7 pm

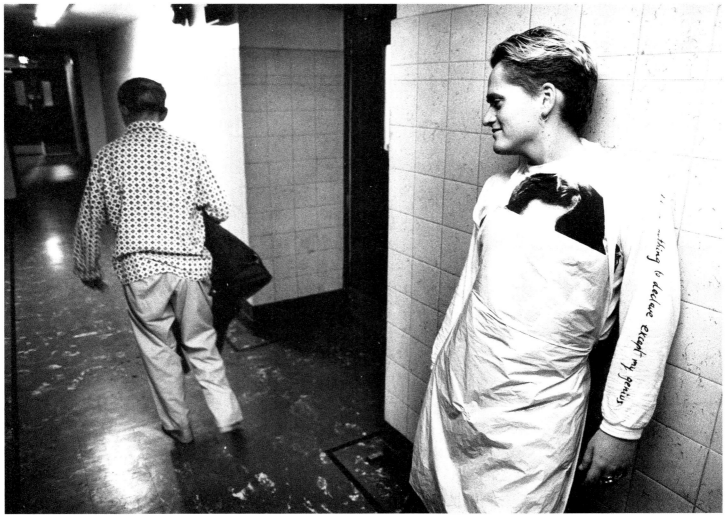

Talbot Centre for the single homeless

MIKE ABRAHAMS

Watching Scotland play Argentina on television in the Horseshoe Bar   8 pm

DAVID MODELL

The band prepare to play before the match 7 pm

Bonnie Scotland – A football fan with Painted face

Two young fans and a police horse see eye-to-eye on the way to Hamden

b169

MARK PETERSON

ALEXANDRA AVAKIAN

On the terracing at the Scotland v Argentina match
which Scotland won 1–0

NIGEL PARRY

DAVID MITCHELL

Bridges over the River Clyde at dusk

EMILE LUIDER

Folk musicians in the Halt Bar

MIKE WILKINSON

Looking east at the City Chambers rooftop from West George Street

DAVID MITCHELL

The Mitchell Library late at night

NEIL LIBBERT

Wildcat Theatre perform at the Tramway where the audience mingles with the performers

performing "John Brown's Body"

NEIL LIBBERT

The Humpff Family perform Cajun music at the Victoria Bar

JOHN DOWNING

These two photographs taken late in the evening
show young Glaswegians doing one of the things
they do best – talking

CHRISTOPHER PILLITZ

THE PHOTOGRAPHERS

Michael Abrahams 1	*Don McPhee 17*
Ron Anderson 2	*Allan Milligan 18*
Marc Asnin 3	*David Mitchell 19*
Alexandra Avakian 4	*David Modell 20*
Ian Berry 5	*Christopher Morris 21*
Lesley Donald 6	*Nigel Parry 22*
John Downing 7	*Mark Peterson 23*
Jillian Edelstein 8	*Christopher Pillitz 24*
Stephen Gibson 9	*John Reardon 25*
Mike Goldwater 10	*David Rose 26*
Robert Gumpert 11	*Glyn Satterley 27*
Ian Hossack 12	*Michel Setboun 28*
Kenneth Jarecke 13	*Tom Stoddart 29*
Neil Libbert 14	*Ian Torrance 30*
Emile Luider 15	*Richard Waite 31*
Gerard McCann 16	*Mike Wilkinson 32*
	John Young 33

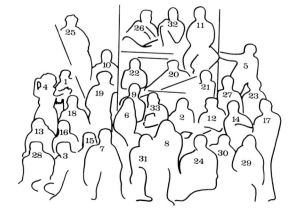

RICHARD WAITE

MICHAEL ABRAHAMS

'A founding member of Network Photographers in 1981, I have been working as a photographer since 1975. I have been widely published in European, American and UK magazines. My major work has been in the Middle East, Africa, Eastern Europe and Northern Ireland as well as social documentary work in the UK. I co-authored the book *Still War* with Laurie Sparham published in 1989.'

RON ANDERSON

'My first job was in the darkroom of the *Scottish Daily Mail*. In the 1960s I joined a Glasgow based photographic agency and was the only photographer at the scene of the Ibrox Disaster. My next job was with the *News of the World* where I stayed for ten years. Then I joined the staff to launch The *Sunday Standard* and was judged the Sports Photographer of the year during this time. After the *Sunday Standard* ceased publication, I worked as a freelance covering main news and sports events for most national newspapers and magazines. I was invited to go to London to be Features Photographer with the London *Daily News* and then joined Robert Maxwell's planning group working on new publications – among them the *European*. Currently I am working on contract covering Scotland for the *Daily Telegraph*.'

MARC ASNIN

Marc received his BFA in photography from the School of Visual Arts in 1985. He was an instructor for the International Center of Photography and Stockton State College from 1985–89. Marc has been a member of JB Pictures for the past two years concentrating on the Youth of America. His pictures have been published in the *Village Voice*, *Essence* Magazine, *Life* Magazine and many other major publications. His honours and awards include National Endowment for the Arts Fellowship 1988, New York Foundation for the Arts Grant 1988, *LIFE* Contest for Young Photographers 1987, the Rhodes Family Award, School of Visual Arts 1985, Society of Newspaper Designers Award of Excellence 1984. He lives in Brooklyn, New York.

ALEXANDRA AVAKIAN

Alexandra graduated from Sarah Lawrence College in 1983 where she studied literature. Next, at the International Center of Photography, she studied photography with Pat Blue and Willis Hartshorn and at the New School for Social Research with Lisette Model and George Tice. During this period she also assisted Bruce Davidson, Ethan Hoffman, Susan Meiselas and Erica Lennard. Her first story was a personal project on a family living in a welfare hotel in Manhattan and was published in the *New York Times*

Magazine in 1985. She then began a personal project on Haiti in February 1986. She made three trips to the island during the next year, totalling five and a half months, supporting herself with assignments from the *New York Times*, the *New York Times* Magazine, *Newsweek*, the US Committee for UNICEF and a grant from the New York Foundation for the Arts. The results of the project were published in the *New York Times* Magazine. In 1987 Alexandra began working in the Middle East for various publications and had the following stories published:

> The West Bank in Jerusalem (the *New York Times* Magazine and *Time* Magazine).
> Yassar Arafat and the PLO (the *New York Times* Magazine 18/12/88).
> The Israeli Army (the *New York Times* Magazine 7/5/89).
> West Bank Settlements – the (*New York Times* Magazine 7/5/89).
> The West Bank – several assignments for *Time* Magazine published in 1988 and 1989.

Alexandra has also covered events in the Soviet Union:

> The Armenian earthquake (*LIFE* magazine December 1988).
> Moscow (a special issue of *Time* magazine in January 1988).
> Azerbijan Unrest (the *New York Times*).
> Moscow Anti-drug Rock Concert (the *New York Times* and *Spin* Magazine).

Armenia One Year After the Earthquake (*Time* Magazine and The *Correspondent*).
in Iran:
> Khomeni's funeral (*Time* Magazine).
in Eastern Europe:
> Berlin and Prague (*LIFE* magazine January 1990).

Alexandra has taken the photographs for *Amish Quilt Country* published by Clarkson Potter in 1989 and for *Rocky Mountain Cooking* published by Clarkson Potter in 1989.
Her work has been shown at Perpignan in an exhibition sponsored by *Paris Match* and *FOTO*.

IAN BERRY

Born on 4 April 1934 in Preston, Lancashire. Ian moved to South Africa in 1952 where he worked for the *Rand Daily Mail* and later the magazine *Drum* until 1960. On moving to Paris in 1962 he became an associate member of Magnum. Later in 1966 he moved to London and worked there on contract for *The Observer Magazine*. In 1967 he became a full member of Magnum. Ian received the first major photographic bursary from the Arts Council of Great Britain in 1974; he was Nikon's Photographer of the Year in 1977. He was elected European vice-president of Magnum in 1976 and 1977. Ian's publications include *The English*. London: Allan Lane, 1978.

JOHN DOWNING

'I left school at fifteen to serve a five year apprenticeship in the Daily Mail dark room. That completed, I freelanced for the *Daily Express* and then was taken on to the staff and have stayed there for the last twenty-six years where I am now chief photographer. I was British Press Photographer of the year in 1971, 1977, 1980, 1981, 1984, 1988 and 1989 and have been twice runner-up in the World Press Competition. I have been awarded the UN gold medal for the Year of the Child and a gold medal for the Photokina Exhibition in Germany. A founder member of the British Press Photographers Association I have been President for three consecutive years. I am Welsh by birth.'

LESLEY DONALD

A graduate of Edinburgh College of Art and Dunfermline College of Physical Education, Lesley has worked as an Arts Recreation Officer for Fife Regional Council; from 1983–86 as a freelance photographer for a Fife News Agency; from 1986–87 as a BBC Publicity/Location Stills Photographer in London and since 1987 as a freelance photographer based in Scotland. When with the BBC she was published in a variety of magazines and as a freelance has had work published in most national Newspapers, the *Radio Times*, *Country Living*, *ES* Magazine, the *Independent* and *Scotland on Sunday*. Most recently she was asked to shoot all the British stills for Prince Charles's BBC documentary *One World*.

JILLIAN EDELSTEIN

Thirty two years old. Client publications include the *Observer* Magazine, the *Independent* Magazine, *Elle*, *Harpers and Queen*, the *Telegraph* Magazine, *GQ*, *7 Days*, the *Sunday Times* Magazine and The *Correspondent* Magazine. Awards include the Photographers' Gallery Portrait Award 1990, Kodak European Award 1989 and the AFAEP Merit Award 1990.

MIKE GOLDWATER

Graduated from Sussex University in 1972 with an Honours BSc in physics. Director of the Half Moon Gallery, London from 1974 to 1980. A trip to the Thai-Cambodian border in November 1979 to cover Khmer refugee situation resulted in his first major spread, published in *NOW!* Magazine. Then followed a trip to Vietnam in 1980 to do a story on the effects of the defoliant Agent Orange and its contaminant dioxin on the Vietnamese people. A grant from the GLAA to photograph the effects of dioxin in the UK resulted in an exhibition which toured for two years with a copy exhibition touring in the USA. In 1981 he co-founded the Network Agency with seven other photographers. Between 1981 and 1990 spent 18 months in Central America covering the situation in El Salvador, Nicaragua, Honduras and Guatemala. In 1984 he began a project on famine in the Sahel which resulted in the book *Fighting the Famine* published by Pluto Press in 1985. He also held a joint exhibition with Chris Steele-Perkins on *Famine in Africa* at the Side Gallery which toured the UK. Since 1986 he has travelled widely covering assignments and doing self-generated stories for UK and foreign magazines. Pictures from a set on Aids in Uganda were highly recommended in the 1987 World Press Awards. He took photographs in Pakistan for the book *Indus Journey* to be published by Chatto & Windus in 1990.

ROBERT GUMPERT

Born in Los Angeles 42 years ago and now living in San Francisco. A freelance since 1974 and with Katz Pictures since 1988. Specialises in social/political and economic topics. Clients include *Der Spiegel*, the *Sunday Times*, *Stern*, The *Economist*, the *Guardian* and the *Los Angeles Times*. Working in black and white only he also does regular work for Oxfam USA, Institution for Food and Development Policy.

IAN HOSSACK

Born 41 years ago in Glasgow he began his career with the *Scottish Daily Mail* which closed in 1968. Then followed a hectic three years in Northern Ireland with the *Belfast Telegraph*. In 1973 he joined the staff of the *Glasgow Herald* where he has stayed ever since. He has won countless awards including the following:

1970 – Irish Features Photographer of the Year
1972 – Runner-up in the Scottish Press Photographer of the Year Awads
1984 – Scottish Press Photographer of the year and Scottish Sports Photographer of the Year
1985 – Winner Sports Picture of the Year
1989 – Scottish winner Open Section SPPY
1990 – Winner Sports Picture of the Year and runner-up Press Photographer of the Year

KENNETH JARECKE

While studying communications at the University of Nebraska in 1982, Kenneth Jarecke launched his photographic career as a freelancer for the Associated Press. For the next few years, he focused on sporting events and the farm crisis in the Midwest. In 1986, he joined Contact Press Images. He immersed himself in the political scene photographing the Iran-contra hearings and gaining access to the usually elusive Oliver North. Since 1987, Jarecke has traveled constantly covering the turmoiled elections in Haiti, a violent Irish Republican Army funeral in Belfast and the Seoul Summer Olympics. His critically acclaimed portfolio for 1988 won him second place for the prestigious "Magazine Photographer of the Year" award. The most published photographer on the American presidential campaign trail, his indepth coverage of George Bush and Jesse Jackson earned him additional Pictures of the Year and World Press Photo prizes. Jarecke continues to move around the world photographing the inauguration of U.S. President George Bush in Washington, D.C., the funeral of Japanese Emperor Hirohito in Tokyo and Calypso music in Trinidad. The publications that his images regularly appear in include *Time*, *Life*, *Forbes*, *U.S. News & World Report*, The London *Sunday Times* Magazine, *Le Figaro*, *Stern* and *Sette*.

NEIL LIBBERT

Has worked as a professional photographer for thirty years, mainly in black and white and clients include newspapers such as the *Observer* and the *Guardian*. Exhibitions on DHSS Supplementary Benefit Offices Projects have included one on DHSS Supplementary Benefit Offices exhibited in the foyer of the National Theatre, London and at the Museum of Modern Art, Oxford in 1989 and one on the Homeless in London exhibited at the Camden Arts Centre in 1989. He was one of the photographers on the book *One Day in the life of Australia* (the first of its kind) published in 1980. Was the winner of the Tom Hopkinson Photojournalist of the Year Award in 1990.

EMILE LUIDER

Born on 7 June 1959 in Ridderkirk, The Netherlands. First photographs taken at the age of sixteen. Studied at The Fine Arts School of Sintjoost, Breda, The Netherlands. In 1984 Emile joined the Rapho Agency in Paris. Highlights in his career to date as follows:

1984 – covered the Venice Carnival

1985 – First assignment for *Geo* Germany, the subject was 'The Rotterdam harbour and its new architecture'

1986 – Awarded first prize in the Art Serie World Press awards

1987/8 – Travelled widely in Togo, Mali, Senegal, India, Canada, Italy, Greece, and Malta on assignments for *Geo, Stern, Sabena Review* and *Merian*

1989 – Travelled in India, Canada and the Netherlands. Published a book on *Arche de la Defense*, Paris. Covered an assignment on La Villette Science Museum for *Geo*

1990 – Awarded first and second prizes in the Art Serie World Press awards

GERARD McCANN

Gerard is a Glasgow based photojournalist whose work on major international stories such as refugees in Sudan, the war in Tigray and the AIDS tragedy in Romania has been widely published. His award winning essay on life behind bars at Barlinnie Prison illustrates his commitment to in-depth projects. He is a founder member of North Star Picture Agency and an associate of Katz pictures.

DON McPHEE

'Aged 45. The first ten years of my working life were spent on provincial newspapers in Manchester, Southend, Norwich and with a news agency in York. I returned to my native Manchester to join the *Guardian* as one of their two Northern-based staff photographers covering an area from the Midlands to Scotland and Ireland. I work in black and white using Nikon and Leica equipment. I have won numerous Ilford photographer of the Year Awards, the Photokina Award and the United Nations Award and am the current British Press Photographer of the Year.'

ALLAN MILLIGAN

Allan has been photographing the life and people of Glasgow for twenty-eight years. He joined the *Scotsman* in May 1962 and is now the paper's chief photographer. Born in Kirkconnel, Dumfriesshire in 1943 he was educated at Sanquhar Academy. At the age of seventeen he joined the *Cumnock Chronicle* as junior photographer. After two years in Cumnock he left to join the *Edinburgh Evening Dispatch*, then spent a short period in Inverness before moving to Glasgow to work for the *Scotsman*, where he has worked ever since. Allan has taken prizes in numerous photographic competitions including the British Photographer of the Year, Scottish Photographer of the Year and Sports Photographer of the Year. Thousands of assignments for the *Scotsman* have included the launch of the QE2, the Ibrox disaster in which 66 people died in the football stadium, the Clarkston gas explosion and the Lockerbie air disaster in December 1988.

DAVID MITCHELL

David has worked as a freelance photojournalist in Scotland for over twenty years. His work appears frequently in national and international publications and his pictures from major events such as the Lockerbie Disaster have taken a number of awards. He is a founder member of North Star Picture Agency.

DAVID MODELL

Age 21. Works mainly in black and white for clients such as the *Independent* Magazine, *ES* magazine, *Stern, 7 Days* and the *Independent on Sunday*. Works for Katz Pictures.

CHRISTOPHER MORRIS

Based in New York Christopher is currently on the staff of the Black Star photographic agency. He came to New York in 1980 from Florida where he received a Bachelor of Science degree in Photography from the Art Institute of Fort Lauderdale. His final semester at the Institute was spent as a news photo-intern with the *Miami Herald*. His move to New York was precipitated by the receipt of a one year scholarship from the International Center of Photography. During his studies at ICP he worked part-time with the Black Star photographic library.

The following year he began working as a stringer for Black Star in New York. He began his foreign photojournalistic work in 1983 with coverage of the anti-nuclear demonstrations in West Germany. In 1984 he made the first of many trips to the Philippines.

In November 1985 Christopher became a Black Star staff photographer. He returned to the Philippines in January 1986 to cover the sudden and impromptu Presidential elections called by President Marcos. Since that time he has made several trips to Central and South America and the Middle East. In 1989 he was in Eastern Europe covering the Czechoslovakian Revolution. He was also in Berlin when the wall came tumbling down. In the same year he recorded the Columbian drug related violence in Medellin and in Afghanistan the Guerilla activities. His coverage of the fire fight during the United States invasion of Panama won him the Second Place Award at the 1990 World Press Photo Contest in the Spot News Stories category. Christopher became a contract photographer for *Time* Magazine in January 1990 and has made several trips to the Soviet Union covering all aspects of change throughout the USSR. Christopher is committed to photojournalistic coverage of history-making events and the use of his camera to help people understand more clearly what is taking place around the world.

NIGEL PARRY

'Born in Yorkshire in 1961. Moved to London after attending Coventry Polytechnic. Attended the London College of Printing but 'bunked off' to join a publishing company. Slid into professional photography after being given a big break by Matthew Evans, the chairman of Faber & Faber, and the Groucho Club. Since then I've been undertaking freelance portrait commissions for various publications such as the *Independent* Magazine, the *Sunday Telegraph* Magazine and the *Sunday Times* Magazine and love every minute of it!'

MARK PETERSON

Mark started his career in photojournalism in his home town of Minneapolis, Minnesota in 1981. He went on to become a staff photographer with United Press International until 1987. At present he works for JB Pictures in New York concentrating on world events and socially significant stories. Mark has been published in all the major news magazines in the United States and Europe.

CHRISTOPHER PILLITZ

Born in Buenos Aires, Argentina in 1958, he travelled to Europe in 1978. After taking a degree in Hotel Management he began his photographic career in 1983 publishing stories on Argentina for the *Observer* and *Sunday Times* Magazines. In 1984 he joined Impact Photos and since then has travelled extensively around the world for leading European and American publications. In 1988 he joined Network Photographers and in 1989 took part in the joint Network Travelling Exhibition on work undertaken in Revolutionary Eastern Europe in 1989.

JOHN REARDON

Born 1951. He spent three years at the Birmingham school of photography although it was not until 1980 that he returned to photography. The following 5 years were spent in Birmingham where he collaborated in Handsworth Self-portrait, an exhibition of portraits of the people of Handsworth, taken by themselves in a free street studio. He was a founder member of *Ten-8* magazine. In 1984 Jonathan Cape published *Home Front* a pictorial record of the lives of those living in multicultural Birmingham. In December 84 the Photographers gallery exhibited the *Home Front* exhibition. Since 1985 he has worked as a Freelance based in London. Works with Katz Pictures.

DAVID ROSE

'Previously freelance mainly with the London *Standard* and the *Guardian*. I joined the *Independent* at its launch and am now with the *Independent on Sunday*. I am based in London.'

GLYN SATTERLEY

Born in Kent Glyn worked in Scotland on various long-term personal projects after leaving Art College in 1975 and has lived in the country since 1982. Much of his personal work has culminated in exhibitions and has been published in several books

including *Life in Caithness and Sutherland*, *Britain's National Parks* and *Trustlands* which reached number one in Scotland's bestseller list in 1989. He is currently completing work on a book on Highland Sporting Estates to be published in Autumn 1990. Although at heart a documentary/landscape photographer after fifteen years experience working on a freelance basis for a variety of European and American magazines such as the *Observer*, The *Independent*, *Departures*, *Country Living*, *Ambiente* and *Condé Nast Traveller*, he has become an extremely versatile photographer adept at producing high quality reportage interiors and portraiture in both colour and black and white.

MICHEL SETBOUN

Born on 27 August 1952 in Bone, Algeria. Studied as an architect, graduating in 1976.

Between 1978 and 1982 Michel worked as a reporter at the SIPA press agency covering major world events such as the struggle for independence in Angola, the revolution in Iran, the Afghan war, the Iran-Iraq war, the conflict in the Lebanon, war in El Salvador and the events in Poland. He was awarded first prize in the World Press Awards for coverage of the plight of refugees in Nigeria. Michel's work has been published in many major international magazines such as *Time*, *Newsweek*, *Stern*, *Bunte*, *Paris Match*, *Geo*, *Life*, *Figaro* and the *Sunday Times*. Between covering these news stories Michel has travelled widely in countries such as Albania, the Yemen, Guatemala, Sweden and Egypt.

After two years on the staff of the Franco-American agency Black Star France, he joined the Rapho Agency in 1985. His work is geared towards long term projects such as South Korea before the Olympic Games, Brazil during the Rio Carnival, Albania, the city of Marseille and Islam in

Europe. In addition to these special projects he regularly works on magazine assignments on various subjects such as portraits, the environment and industry. He has participated in several group exhibitions in Paris, Amsterdam, Vienna and Perpignan and was one of the photographers who worked on the book *Trois Jours En France* published by Nathan Image in 1989.

TOM STODDART

Born in Morpeth, Northumberland thirty six years ago Tom lives in Dulwich, London. He has worked for a number of daily newspapers including the *Daily Express* and *Today* before joining the *Sunday Times*.

In 1988 he joined *7 Days* Magazine leaving in May 1989 to join Katz Pictures. He is currently working on major news and feature stories for international magazines such as the *Sunday Times*, *Stern*, *Time*, the *Telegraph* and the *Sunday Correspondent*. Assignments recently covered include the fall of the Berlin Wall, the Romanian Revolution, child labour in India and Eton School 1990.

IAN TORRANCE

Born in Edinburgh in 1940. Served for fifteen years with the *Daily Express* in Edinburgh from 1958–74, first as darkroom boy then photographer. In May 1974 he joined the *Daily Record* in Glasgow and became chief photographer for the paper in 1977. Ian has won many major awards in news, sport, royal and features categories over the last twenty five years including the Scottish Press Photographer of the Year in 1978 and 1989 and British Regional Press Photographer of the Year in 1978 and 1979. He was the British Photographer of the Year in 1979.

RICHARD WAITE

Age 36. Works mainly in large format for clients such as the *Sunday Times* Magazine, the *Observer* Magazine, the weekend *Telegraph* Magazine, *7 Days* and *Architects and Designers*. His awards include D & A D poster award and the Sun Life award.

MIKE WILKINSON

Born in 1962 in Leeds he studied on the BA Photographic Studies course at Napier College in Edinburgh. In 1987 he achieved a degree pass with commendation. Whilst at college he was awarded an Agfa bursary to develop ideas on Impressionistic colour photography which resulted in an exhibition at the National Theatre, London in 1987. Mike taught photography at summer camp in Massachusetts, USA in 1987 and produced photographic documentation of the camp in the form of a yearbook. Since 1988 he has lived in Glasgow but travelled extensively throughout Scotland on wide ranging assignments for the *Times* and the *Sunday Times*.

JOHN YOUNG

Born in 1963 in Glasgow he trained in photojournalism at Richmond College, Sheffield. He joined the *Helensburgh Advertiser* in May 1984. While working for this newspaper he was highly commended in the 1984 Scottish Press Photographer of the Year competition (portfolio) and a runner-up in the Provincial Photographer of the Year and Young Photographer of the Year awards. In 1986 he was awarded the NCJJ Photographer of the Year title, and in 1986 he joined the staff of the *Glasgow Evening Times*. In March 1989 he was named Scottish Photographer of the Year for 1988.

Mike Wilkinson

The end of a perfect day. Good night